COMPANION OF:

_____

THE
MINDFUL
TRAVELER

Exploration Journal

THIS JOURNAL WAS CREATED FOR TRAVELERS who wish to cultivate mindfulness and experience every day with intention while on the road.

Like any book or story, your adventure moves through stages, from start to end. *The Mindful Traveler* is divided into sections that guide you through these phases as you move through your journey.

The first section helps you prepare and adjust to a period of travel, encouraging you to relish your excitement, release your stress, and care for yourself in ways that are sometimes forgotten.

The second section invites you to experience your world in new ways through a series of prompts and meditations designed to help you reflect on your adventures and invite you to enjoy the present moment at its fullest.

The third section creates a sense of peace and closure at the end of your trip and sends you home with a heart full of the friends you've made, the adventures you've had, and the lasting memories you've created.

You can use the fourth section daily throughout your trip to describe your destinations, set daily intentions, and reflect on your thoughts and adventures.

May your travels be joyful, peaceful, challenging, and stimulating, and may the adventure continue for the rest of your life.

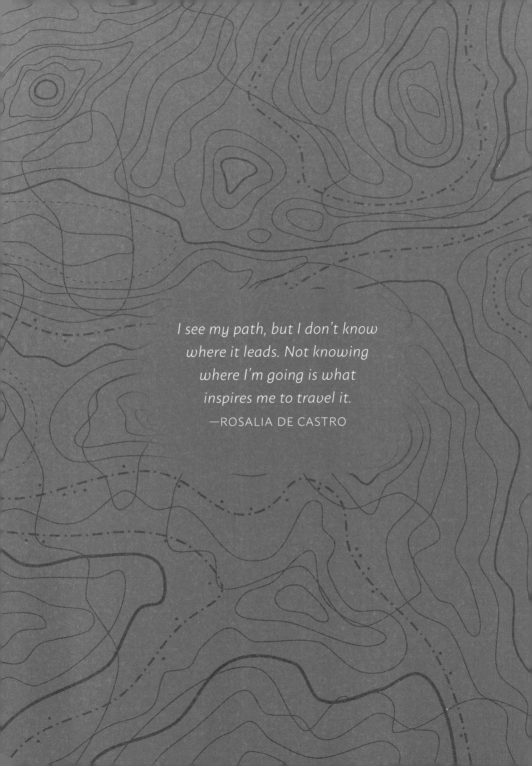

I see my path, but I don't know where it leads. Not knowing where I'm going is what inspires me to travel it.
—ROSALIA DE CASTRO

THE START OF IT ALL

AT YOUR PLACE OF DEPARTURE

Departure is, in many ways, a point of no return. You'll have forgotten some things and run out of time for others. You might be rethinking a destination, a method of travel, or even your traveling companion. Maybe you're terrified to be going out on your own. You're probably experiencing excitement, nervousness, regret, or—hopefully—release. There is nothing you can change now. For better or worse, this is the start of your adventure. Give yourself one last check for the three things you can't (easily) replace on the way—passport or ID, ticket, and money—and reassure yourself that the rest you can buy, borrow, or do without. Take this space to write your hopes, ideas, worries, fears—anything that comes to mind. Congratulations. This is it.

TRIP INTENTION

Create an itinerary of **EXPERIENCES** you could have on this trip that aren't tied to a specific destination. Try to do all of these things in your travels.

Turn down an unassuming street and find something magical.

Get out of a stressful situation using your own skills and willpower.

Make a life-changing connection.

Create a list of **UNFORESEEN EVENTS** that you're afraid might happen in your travels. Remember that challenging experiences are part of the adventure, and allow yourself to embrace the unexpected, both good and bad. Close your eyes and picture each of these worries dissolving in acceptance of the present moment. Life is unpredictable and full of the unknown—and sometimes that's the beauty of it.

Take bad advice.

Get lost in an unfamiliar area.

Lose something important.

Release yourself from any feelings of "should" or "need to" today. **ALLOW YOURSELF TO DO ONLY WHAT FEELS GOOD.**

How was it? Did you feel like you were missing out? Were you able to lovingly accept yourself and your wants throughout the day?

Remember that travel is about **FULFILLING YOURSELF,** not checking things off a list. Give yourself permission to take obligation-free days when you want and need.

Pick a ritual that you traditionally practice at home,
such as your morning routine or a self-care habit,
and recreate it on your trip.

Pay attention to what feels different and what feels
the same. Consider how the change of circumstances
brings a new dimension to this practice.

Engage in a **CONVERSATION** with someone you met while traveling. Draw the person you spoke to. List adjectives to describe them, and other words about your exchange. No need to try to recreate the dialogue. Appreciate the fleeting nature of your time with this person.

Take ten minutes for yourself sometime during your adventures today.
Sit quietly on your own. Slow your breathing and close your eyes.
Check in with your body. Are you sore? Are you tired?
Is your body grateful for the exercise you've been
giving it while moving from place to place?

Now check in with your mind. Travel is often busy, and it's easy to miss the
emotions we're experiencing. Maybe you're feeling joy and excitement.
Take time to pause with those feelings and enjoy the experience.
Or perhaps you're overwhelmed. Allow yourself to feel that way,
and consider whether you'd benefit from some downtime.

Pick a place you've passed by that looks interesting. Below, speculate on what this place is like, and who the people inside it are. Tell a story about this place. Promise yourself you'll visit it while you're here.

When you do, come back to this page and reflect on what it was really like. Was it anything like what you anticipated? Do you see ways in which your speculations influenced your real-life experience at this place? Consider how preconceived ideas can **ALTER YOUR VIEW** of reality.

List some affirmations about yourself. Return to them when you're nervous,
stressed, or lonely in your travels.

I am powerful.

I am a valuable friend and ally.

I am able to adapt to meet the challenges presented to me.

Eat a typical dish from the area you're traveling through.
Focus deeply on each bite. Savor the smells, flavors, and textures
of this food. Pay attention to how your body reacts to it.
Allow yourself to feel gratitude that, among the infinite possibilities in the
universe, you are able to be here and present for this experience.

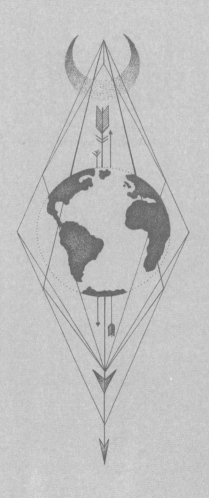

Windows provide a slice of life outside—an incomplete picture of the world around you. Sit by a window and draw what you see.

DESCRIBE THE VIEW. What can you tell about the place you're in? What important details might you be missing? Consider how much more there is to experience in this place than you'll ever be able to. Seek acceptance of this fact, and gratitude for all the experiences you will have here.

There are so many things to do when you visit a new place, but there's never enough time to do them all. Instead of trying to fit everything in, try to live in the moment and get the most out of what you're doing at the time. Fill this whole page with a tightly wound spiral, with each line almost touching the last. Draw it slowly and ever so carefully, and the whole time keep your mind focused on the spiral. Realize that this task is going to take however long it takes. GRANT IT PATIENCE AND ATTENTION. If your mind wanders, gently bring it back to this task. There are an infinite number of other things you could be doing at this moment, but you have chosen this.

Sometimes during your travels, you will find yourself feeling melancholy. While sadness is a lonely feeling, melancholy is the feeling of connection to all of humanity—to everyone who's felt the same things you're feeling and to the human condition that all people share. It's natural to feel melancholy while traveling: you're connecting to a world full of other people with their own hardships and sorrows. Allow yourself to hold this feeling of melancholy close, and accept it with kind, open arms.

What was your biggest culture shock?
Let out all your thoughts and feelings about it here.

Wherever you go,
go with all your heart.
—CONFUCIUS

THE GRAND ADVENTURE

Pick a direction. Walk that way. Get a little lost. Take whichever turns strike you. Find an activity along the way. Eat somewhere unassuming.

What did you do? What was this experience like in comparison to your everyday?

Find a song about the city or area you're currently in.
Listen to it in the morning and let the musician's passion inspire
and inform you throughout your day exploring this place.

Go a day without recording your experiences in photos or on social media.
Ponder the sensation of living a day that is kept completely to your present self.

_____

_____

_____

_____

_____

_____

_____

_____

_____

_____

_____

_____

_____

_____

_____

_____

_____

_____

_____

_____

_____

_____

_____ Was it challenging? Did you find

_____ yourself anxious about missing a

_____ shot or an opportunity to connect?

_____ Did this exercise change your

_____ experience?

Find a green space, like a park or garden. Sit down and close your eyes. Let your hands fall comfortably in your lap. Breathe slowly and intentionally, focusing on each breath. Notice when involuntary thoughts distract you, and allow them to pass without judgment. When you're in a comfortable rhythm within yourself, cast your awareness outwards to the space around you. What is different from the sounds you hear at home? What is the same?

Is your body or mind telling you something today?
Perhaps you need better food, more exercise,
a good night's sleep, or some loving kindness.
Trust your intuition about what you need, and follow it.

A loving kindness meditation:

This is a moment of suffering that is destined to pass.

*I will be kind to myself and remember
that all feelings are transient.*

SAY YES TO AN INVITATION.

What happened? How will this experience affect your decision next time you receive an invitation like this? Remember that both positive and negative experiences are of value to you, and let your thoughts about the excursion flow freely onto the page. Don't worry about how your words sound—just keep your pen moving until you reach the end of the page.

Travel can leave us feeling free and relaxed in a way that's hard to find in day-to-day life. Take a moment to pause on a good feeling. Notice what parts of your body are affected, and what thoughts it brings forward in your mind. Consider other times you've felt like this and think about ways you can create this feeling for yourself.

LIST EXPERIENCES FROM TODAY
THAT YOU'RE GRATEFUL FOR.

THEN LIST SOME THINGS THAT
YOU'RE NOT GRATEFUL FOR.

Try to find gratitude in some form within the experiences featured in the second list. Perhaps they challenged you to deal with difficult emotions or gave you the ability to fix something when it goes wrong in the future. Working through this process is easier said than done, and you won't necessarily succeed today. Be patient with yourself as you take important steps in this challenging process.

It may not feel like it in the moment, but you will forget so much of this trip. Pick an experience from today (maybe it's happening now?) that you don't expect to remember in a month, and write about it in detail.

Draw something about it, too. This act may cement this memory in your head, or it may only come back to you when you reread this journal.

Describe an interaction you've had on this trip with someone who touched your soul.
WHAT ABOUT THIS PERSON ENDEARED THEM TO YOU?

_____

_____

_____

_____

_____

_____

_____

_____

_____

_____

_____

_____

_____

_____

_____

_____

_____

_____

_____

_____

_____

_____

_____

_____   Appreciate that, of all the

_____   people in this place, you had

_____   the chance to meet this one.

Sit comfortably in a museum or another busy
tourist destination, and take ten minutes to be still.
Let your hands fall to your lap. Close your eyes.
Notice everything that happens in these quiet moments.
Is your breathing slow and even?
Can you feel your heart beating through your
chest or down to your fingertips?
Does your back hurt after a while, or
does the weight of your body feel good?
Allow yourself to feel grounded through your seat,
connected to the Earth and the other humans around you.
Appreciate your ability to create these moments of calm
in the midst of the busyness around you.

Are you homesick? What do you miss about home? Without judgment, allow yourself to feel homesick when you do, and let it fill you with gratitude that you have so many good things to yearn for.

What do you think you'll someday miss about the place you're in now?
Encourage yourself to live in the moment when you can.

On this page, draw a destination you plan to travel to later in your trip that you've only seen in pictures.

After you visit, come back to this page and draw it as you've now seen it. Record whatever stands out the most in your head—it doesn't need to be the same view as you drew before. What surprised you? What was as expected?

Travel can get so busy that you forget to make time to check in with yourself. Take a few minutes to listen to your thoughts and emotions now. What is occupying your mind? Write it out as it comes to you. Avoid passing judgment on these thoughts; just relay them as an impartial narrator would.

Travel can be lonely, stressful, and overwhelming just as much as it can be exciting, magical, and fulfilling. On some days it's hard to find gratitude in your experiences; on others it's easy. Whichever type of day this is, list the things that made you smile today.

Draw something beautiful you can see
from where you are now.

Surrender yourself to nature and dedicate today to
honoring the weather. Is it rainy? Hole up in a cozy café
and read with a steaming latte. Is it sunny? Go for a bike
ride and sit by a river or lake. Relish in the loss of
control in an otherwise-regimented life.

It's easy to get overwhelmed or too caught up in planning while you travel, and that can cause you to miss out on the present. Draw something from the PRESENT MOMENT. Don't skimp on the details.

Find a historic site that inspires you. Take a half hour to sit and meditate there. Reflect on the events that took place here and think about the emotions and lives of those who have been here before you. Think about the ways in which human connection can transcend the bounds of time.

Impermanence is a big part of travel. It often informs your actions, connections, and feelings as friendships and experiences slip away. Letting go can be a hard part of normal life, which is more stable and consistent than life on a trip. Nevertheless, letting go creates some beautiful things: worry-free friendships, spontaneous side trips, and the boldness to do things you normally wouldn't. How are you grateful for impermanence on this trip? What have those fleeting experiences created in your life?

Have you encountered anyone with very different beliefs from your own? Is this belief difficult for you to accept? How does it challenge your existing beliefs? If you haven't encountered this, does it surprise you to find people with such similar worldviews here?

Make today about healthy consumption.
Feed yourself only what nourishes both your body and soul.
Listen to uplifting music, and read what makes you grow.
Begin and end each activity with gratitude,
and resolve to learn something from every interaction.

Find somewhere full of everyday life, away from the tourist track.
Draw this place and try to imagine what life is like here.

Travel is often a time of reflection. Have you been thinking of a particular person on this trip? Write a letter to them here. Feel no pressure to send it. If you haven't been thinking of someone, write a letter to yourself about your reflections.

When you come back to your bed in the evening filled
with exhilaration from the day's activities, hold onto that feeling
in meditation before you sleep. Let it bubble inside you as you
keep your body still, channeling all the energy from that feeling
into your heart and soul. Tuck a little bit of it away for the next
day you need a pick-me-up.

Who is the first person you met in the place you're currently in? How did that interaction affect your opinion of the place? Has it changed since? Consider the impact of first impressions on your experiences, and BE MINDFUL of the first impression others will have of you.

Draw a scene from a dream you've had while traveling.

Write some words about the tone of the dream or the feelings it evoked.
How does the dream relate to your waking life?

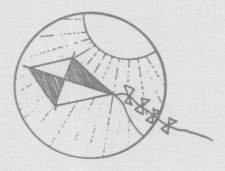

You will often seek help from others during your travels, asking for suggestions, directions, or advice. Invite more generosity into your life today by finding a way to help someone. Do it graciously, without expecting reciprocity or gratitude. Notice how this makes you feel. You are powerful and able to make a difference.

Reflect on a missed opportunity from this trip. Why did you miss it?
What do you think would have happened if you hadn't?

Fill out these pages when you're having a challenging day. Draw whatever you feel: angry scribbles, lethargic waves, sorrowful lines. If the mood strikes you, write about what went wrong. SOMETIMES A DAY IS CHALLENGING DESPITE NOTHING GOING WRONG. IN SOME WAYS, THIS CAN BE EVEN HARDER.

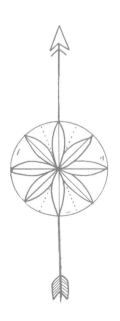

As you walk from one place to another today, keep your
eyes low to the ground. Notice the texture and color of the
ground beneath your feet: how it changes, what it holds.
Use this exercise to connect to the Earth itself,
feeling grounded in your place in the world.

List the things you were given today and by what or whom. Don't just include physical objects: Were you given compassion? An experience? A listening ear? Include the unwanted gifts too, like impatience or bad directions—but don't dwell on them. It's all part of the experience.

What has been the most challenging or stressful part of this trip so far? Without judgment or pressure to change, notice how you feel while recounting this. How were you able to get through the experience? REMEMBER THAT YOU ARE A RESOURCEFUL PERSON, ABLE TO HELP YOURSELF AND OTHERS EVEN WHEN OVERWHELMED.

The days can often pass quickly in travel—as can relationships with the people you meet along the way. Take the time to express a thank you that would usually be left unsaid: "Thank you for sharing your unique sense of humor with me in a stressful time" or "Thank you for reminding me to be grateful."

Draw something you saw today that filled you with wonder.
Try to capture that feeling of awe in your drawing.

What do you have access to that the people around you in this city or country don't?
What kind of advantages and disadvantages do you have because of this?

Sit or lie down and check in with your body.

Pay attention to what feels relaxed and
what feels tense. Does anything hurt?

Have you been eating well and giving yourself the
energy you need for this trip?

Find gratitude for this body and all the places it can take you.

Don't forget to care for it throughout your travels.

List the things that have surprised you about the place you're visiting.

Draw the room or area you're in now. Notice details you wouldn't normally see. Try to capture the light and feel of the place as you're experiencing it now.

During which moment on this trip have you felt most at peace? Describe this feeling, and recall it when you need to relax. Remember that feelings come and go, and this cherished feeling will return, too.

At some point today, take off your shoes and walk barefoot for a while. Let the contact of your feet on the ground remind you of your connection to the Earth and to others. Feel how your body shifts to keep your balance and carry you most efficiently. Let this practice make you feel strong and stable, able to support yourself even as the Earth turns under your feet.

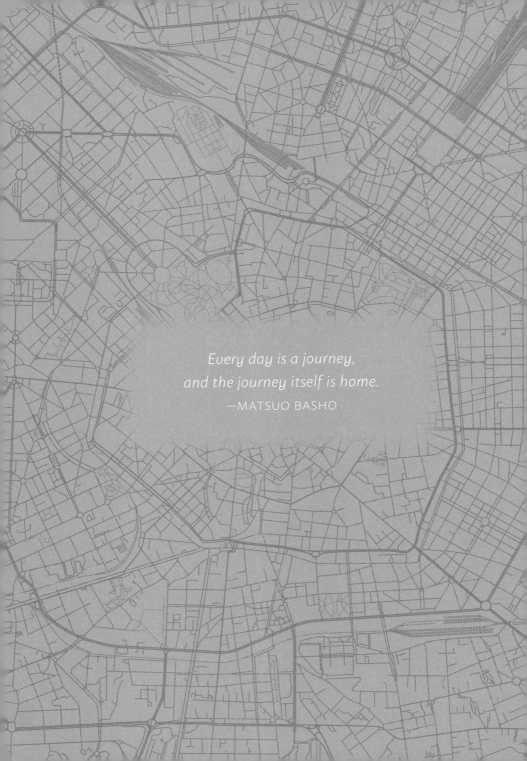

Every day is a journey,
and the journey itself is home.
—MATSUO BASHO

THE JOURNEY HOME

Reflect on the intention you set for yourself on page 7 at the beginning of your trip. How did it emerge in your travels?

_____

_____

_____

_____

_____

_____

_____

_____

_____

_____

_____

_____

_____

_____

_____

_____

_____

_____

_____

_____

_____

_____

_____

_____

_____

_____

_____

_____

If you had to assign your trip a theme, what would it be? How did this theme appear throughout your trip? Did it affect or inform your choices and experiences? Your travel intention may have been the theme, but often something else emerges from the unexpected feelings and events that arise in your travels.

We can't take everything home with us when we travel—and sometimes we don't want to. What have you left behind during this trip? How does it feel to surrender these things? They can be objects, like books or clothing, or emotions, like worry, fear, and stress.

What was the best conversation you had on this journey? Who was it with?
What made it so good? What will you take away from this interaction?

What inspired you on this trip? What has that prompted you to do or change in your everyday life?

What's one tradition or custom you value from the culture you're visiting?
Why do you like this? How could you recreate this experience or the feelings
it evokes once you're home?

Self-care can often fall off the priority list in the midst of work, family, school, and other obligations. Think about the rituals you've developed on this trip that leave you feeling happy, relaxed, and healthy. Choose one to practice daily at home. Maybe it's making time for a nice cup of coffee in the morning, meditating daily, or writing in your journal before bed. Continue to perform this ritual throughout your travels, and practice it the first day you're home and beyond. Turn this newly found habit into an organic part of your life, not just a part of your trip.

What experience from your trip do you expect to remember forever?

What has challenged you most on this trip? What skills or resources did you develop to better deal with situations like this? Are they applicable to other challenges you face in life?

Take some time to reflect on the person or people you're traveling with. If you are traveling alone, consider yourself. Have they surprised you, or have you surprised yourself? Were these surprises challenging at all to receive? (If you have any venting to do about your traveling companions, now would be a good time.) As you get to know people in the future, remember the depth a single person holds and gently remind yourself not to make assumptions.

How do you know you're getting close to "home" in a place you're visiting?
Are there people or things that have become familiar guides to you in your time here?
Draw these personal landmarks here before you leave.

You probably know your way around this place pretty well now. Reflect on your first day here and how unfamiliar everything felt, and on all the things that have happened here since.

What do you wish you could change about your trip? Use this space to release your emotion around these things and to seek love and acceptance of the way your journey turned out.

_____

_____

_____

_____

_____

_____

_____

_____

_____

_____

_____

_____

_____

_____

_____

_____

_____

_____

_____

_____

_____

_____

_____

_____

If you could go back and give yourself advice at the beginning of this trip, what would you say?

Take ten minutes to check in with yourself. How are you feeling as your trip is drawing to an end? Sad? Fearful? Relieved? Excited? Is there anything you've been suppressing or trying to avoid thinking about? Confront those thoughts and feelings now, then practice releasing them in the sprit of self-acceptance.

A loving acceptance meditation:

Breathing in, I welcome calm and peace.
Breathing out, I dispel my fears and expectations.

Reflecting on regrets can be painful, but it's also an important way to grow toward acceptance. What's something you felt was important but didn't have the opportunity to do on this trip? Why didn't you do it? Write about what you were able to do instead with the time or resources you would have dedicated to this activity, and reflect on what you learned from this exchange of experiences. Notice the emotions that come up as you write, but don't try to change or suppress them.

What are you looking forward to about going home? Are there things you'll appreciate more than you did before you left? What fun or fulfilling things are you going to do when you return?

_____

_____

_____

_____

_____

_____

_____

_____

_____

_____

_____

_____

_____

_____

_____

_____

_____

_____

_____

_____

_____

_____

_____

_____

_____

_____

_____

What changes are you going to make when you're home?
Where did these decisions come from?

WHAT PARTS OF YOUR TRIP ARE YOU
MOST EAGER TO TELL OTHERS ABOUT?

WHAT PARTS WILL YOU KEEP
TO YOURSELF?

Use this space to let your thoughts flow freely onto the page, trying not to worry about how it sounds. Reflect on your trip, or your journey home, or the great sandwich you're eating. Let your mind steer itself and nurture an accepting space for your thoughts.

As you wait to depart, practice one last meditation. Close your eyes, let your body relax, and place your hand on the bag you've carried with you throughout this journey. Instead of clothes and material things, picture it full of the experiences you've had on your trip:

Every place or custom that tugged at your heart,
every challenging and magical adventure,
every moment spent in blissful solitude or captivating company,
and every instance of overcoming hesitation or fear to transcend your limits.

Today you'll bring home with you each of these things and you'll carry them with you for the rest of your life. You are not the same version of yourself who set out on this journey. Days, weeks, or maybe months of new experiences have redefined you, strengthened you, and filled your soul.

And you created all of this.

*Traveling—it leaves you speechless,
then turns you into a storyteller.*

—IBN BATTUTA

INTENTIONS AND REFLECTIONS

Here are some sample intentions for those days
when you need a little inspiration.

Be bold.

Connect with others.

Venture out of my comfort zone.

Help someone.

Reflect on things in my life that are hard to confront.

Try new things.

Find gratitude, even when things are hard.

Say yes.

Immerse myself in the culture around me.

Accept what I can't change.

Only make a decision when I am able to think clearly about it.

Love, acknowledge, and accept difficult thoughts when they arise.

Connect with the new natural landscape around me.

Be open and receptive.

Think before I react.

Embody the traits I admire in others.

Forgive myself and others.

Meditate at every pause.

Be still in my mind and heart.

Avoid all forms of escapism (reading, electronics) and live in the moment.

Care for my body.

Care for my soul.

Express my creativity.

Begin and end each activity with gratitude.

LOCATION

DATE

INTENTION

REFLECTION

LOCATION

DATE

INTENTION

REFLECTION

LOCATION ————————————————————————————————

DATE ————————————————————————————————

INTENTION ————————————————————————————————

REFLECTION ————————————————————————————————

LOCATION

DATE

INTENTION

REFLECTION

LOCATION

DATE

INTENTION

REFLECTION

LOCATION _____

DATE _____

INTENTION _____

REFLECTION _____

_____

_____

_____

_____

_____

_____

_____

_____

_____

_____

_____

_____

_____

_____

_____

_____

_____

_____

_____

_____

_____

_____

LOCATION

DATE

INTENTION

REFLECTION

LOCATION ———————————————————————————

DATE ————————————————————————————————

INTENTION ————————————————————————————

REFLECTION ———————————————————————————

LOCATION ———————————————————————————

DATE ———————————————————————————

———————————————————————————————

INTENTION ———————————————————————————

———————————————————————————————

REFLECTION ———————————————————————————

———————————————————————————————
———————————————————————————————
———————————————————————————————
———————————————————————————————
———————————————————————————————
———————————————————————————————
———————————————————————————————
———————————————————————————————
———————————————————————————————
———————————————————————————————
———————————————————————————————
———————————————————————————————
———————————————————————————————
———————————————————————————————
———————————————————————————————
———————————————————————————————
———————————————————————————————
———————————————————————————————
———————————————————————————————
———————————————————————————————
———————————————————————————————
———————————————————————————————
———————————————————————————————
———————————————————————————————

LOCATION

DATE

INTENTION

REFLECTION

LOCATION

DATE

INTENTION

REFLECTION

LOCATION

DATE

INTENTION

REFLECTION

LOCATION

DATE

INTENTION

REFLECTION

LOCATION ——————————————————————————————

DATE ————————————————————————————————

INTENTION ——————————————————————————————

REFLECTION ——————————————————————————————

LOCATION

DATE

INTENTION

REFLECTION

LOCATION

DATE

INTENTION

REFLECTION

LOCATION

DATE

INTENTION

REFLECTION

LOCATION —————————————————————————————

DATE —————————————————————————————————

INTENTION ————————————————————————————

REFLECTION ———————————————————————————

LOCATION ———————————————————————————————

DATE ————————————————————————————————————

INTENTION ——————————————————————————————

REFLECTION —————————————————————————————

LOCATION

DATE

INTENTION

REFLECTION

LOCATION

DATE

INTENTION

REFLECTION

LOCATION ——————————————————————————————————

DATE ——————————————————————————————————————

INTENTION —————————————————————————————————

REFLECTION ————————————————————————————————

LOCATION ————————————————————————————————————

DATE ————————————————————————————————————

INTENTION ————————————————————————————————————

REFLECTION ————————————————————————————————————

LOCATION _____

DATE _____

INTENTION _____

REFLECTION _____

_____

_____

_____

_____

_____

_____

_____

_____

_____

_____

_____

_____

_____

_____

_____

_____

_____

_____

_____

_____

_____

_____

LOCATION

DATE

INTENTION

REFLECTION

LOCATION

DATE

INTENTION

REFLECTION

LOCATION

DATE

INTENTION

REFLECTION

LOCATION _____

DATE _____

INTENTION _____

REFLECTION _____

_____

_____

_____

_____

_____

_____

_____

_____

_____

_____

_____

_____

_____

_____

_____

_____

_____

_____

_____

_____

_____

_____

_____

_____

LOCATION ————————————————————————————————————

DATE ————————————————————————————————————

INTENTION ————————————————————————————————————

REFLECTION ————————————————————————————————————

LOCATION ———————————————————————————————

DATE ———————————————————————————————

INTENTION ———————————————————————————————

REFLECTION ———————————————————————————————

LOCATION

DATE

INTENTION

REFLECTION

LOCATION

DATE

INTENTION

REFLECTION

LOCATION

DATE

INTENTION

REFLECTION

LOCATION

DATE

INTENTION

REFLECTION

LOCATION

DATE

INTENTION

REFLECTION

LOCATION _____

DATE _____

INTENTION _____

REFLECTION _____

_____

_____

_____

_____

_____

_____

_____

_____

_____

_____

_____

_____

_____

_____

_____

_____

_____

_____

_____

LOCATION

DATE

INTENTION

REFLECTION

LOCATION ————————————————————————————————

DATE ————————————————————————————————————

INTENTION ———————————————————————————————

REFLECTION ——————————————————————————————

LOCATION —————————————————————————————

DATE —————————————————————————————

INTENTION —————————————————————————————

REFLECTION —————————————————————————————

LOCATION _____

DATE _____

INTENTION _____

REFLECTION _____

_____

_____

_____

_____

_____

_____

_____

_____

_____

_____

_____

_____

_____

_____

_____

_____

_____

_____

_____

_____

_____

_____

_____

LOCATION ———————————————————————————————

DATE ———————————————————————————————

INTENTION ———————————————————————————————

REFLECTION ———————————————————————————————

LOCATION

DATE

INTENTION

REFLECTION

LOCATION

DATE

INTENTION

REFLECTION

LOCATION ——

DATE ———

INTENTION ———————————————————————————————————————

REFLECTION ——————————————————————————————————————

LOCATION —————————————————————————————

DATE —————————————————————————————————

INTENTION ————————————————————————————

REFLECTION ———————————————————————————

MANDALA
PUBLISHING

An Imprint of MandalaEarth
PO Box 3088
San Rafael, CA 94912
www.MandalaEarth.com

Find us on Facebook: www.facebook.com/MandalaEarth
Follow us on Twitter: @MandalaEarth

ISBN: 978-1-68383-409-0

Publisher: Raoul Goff
Associate Publisher: Phillip Jones
Art Director: Chrissy Kwasnik
Designers: Yousef Ghorbani & Chrissy Kwasnik
Senior Editor: Rossella Barry
Associate Managing Editor: Lauren LePera
Editorial Assistant: Tessa Murphy
Senior Production Editor: Rachel Anderson
Production Manager: Sadie Crofts

Text by Tessa Murphy
Illustrations by Eva Svartaur

Mandala Publishing, in association with Roots of Peace, will plant two trees for each tree used in the
manufacturing of this book. Roots of Peace is an internationally renowned humanitarian organization
dedicated to eradicating land mines worldwide and converting war-torn lands into productive farms and
wildlife habitats. Roots of Peace will plant two million fruit and nut trees in Afghanistan and provide
farmers there with the skills and support necessary for sustainable land use.

Manufactured in China by Insight Editions

10 9 8 7 6 5 4 3 2 1

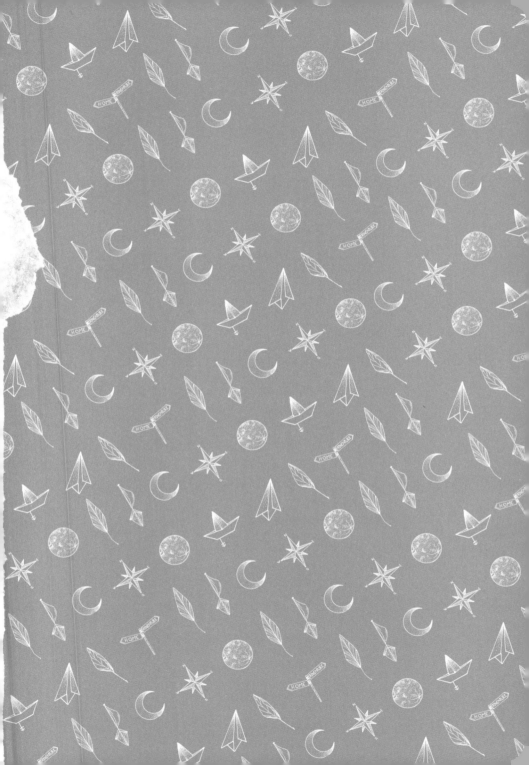

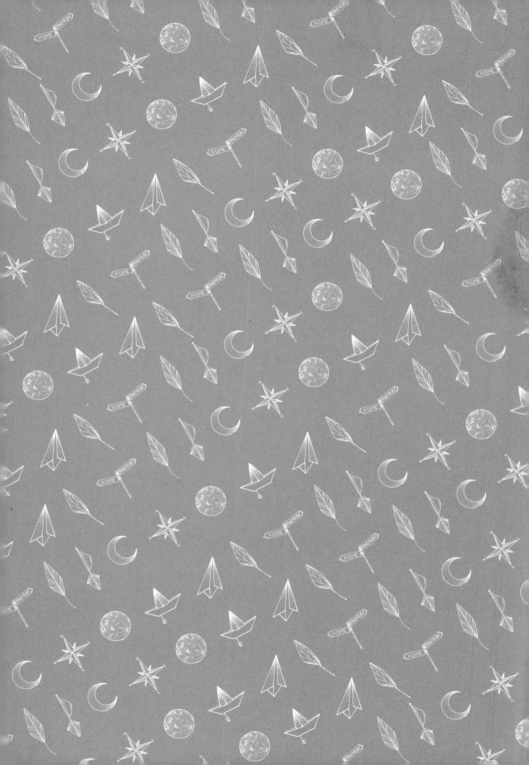